THE POINT BOATS:

THE EXPORT OF COAL FROM THE POINT OF AYR, NORTH WALES

BY W. KEN DAVIES

There are three kinds of people:
the Living,
the Dead,
and those who go to sea.

Dr. Samuel Johnson

This book is dedicated to my late father
and all the seafarers of his generation,
who gave so much for so little.

ACKNOWLEDGEMENTS

Thanks are owed to many people who made this booklet possible. The help of my namesake, Dr. Ken Davies, and the encouragement of Paul Evans, Bryn Jones, Paul Parry, and Gareth Calvely have been invaluable. The kindness of very many people in allowing me to use their photographs of the ships, and the members of their family who sailed them, has added greatly to its historical value, and cannot be overstated. The quality of some reproductions do not match their value asa historical record, and I hope readers will forgive their use in the same spirit. In a similar vein, my own drawings andpaintings are used for their utility rather than their aesthetic qualities.

Most of the crew members are now with us only in memory, but I was privileged to know many of them as my father's shipmates and friends. Their yarns, fascinated me, and I never regretted following in their footsteps to the sea.

Paradoxically, neither did I regret 'swallowing the anchor.' At Coleg Harlech, the late Dr. Lewis Lloyd, Dr. Neil Evans, and Dr. David Wiltshire passed on more formal approaches to history. University taught me the mysteries of research and writing up the results, and particular thanks in this respect are owed to Dr. W.T.R. Rees, my supervisor when working for the Open University.

Making my writing accessible beyond Academia was learned with the help of Mair DeGare-Pitt, Chris Torrance, Eric Morgan, Annie Wilton-Jones, and Mike Byrne. Thanks are owed to them all, and any failings in what follows are entirely my responsibility.

W.Ken Davies. March 2021.

CONTENTS

INTRODUCTION

The remains of the Point of Ayr Harbour are near the most northerly point of mainland Wales, on the Coastal path, about a half mile south of the Point of Ayr Lighthouse. It is on the water's edge of the site of the Point of Ayr Colliery,which was, for over a century, the most prominent economic feature of the ancient parish of Llanasa. Coal exports from the Colliery commenced with the opening of the first seam in 1890. An existing wharf was available, and ships had used the Point of Ayr at least as early as 1650, probably to load Coal from the Picton pits.

The date may well be 200 years earlier. The historic Picton Pool is mentioned by the early historian,Elis Gruffydd,in his account of the role of Ithel Fychan in the fifteenth century Wars of the Roses. It is thought to have been sited at the Point. If so,coal had left there in Tudor times. Indeed, Norse traders probably beached their vessels nearby, and Gwespyr stone may have been transhipped by the Romans to Prestatyn to build the Bathhouse, the remains of which are preserved in Melyd Avenue.

This little volume skips through those early times, offering a little detail on their bearing on the history of the estuary, and the shipping that may have visited the area around the Point of Ayr. It goes on to focus on the development of the coastline and the harbour from the eighteenth century onward. Records from censuses are used to gain a picture of trade during the nineteenth and early twentieth centuries.

Thereafter, the work of maritime historians is drawn upon to discuss the ships and companies which took the coal away from the Point of Ayr. Census records are extremely useful in this respect, as they contain a host of detail about both owners and crews. History is about people, and there is something quite compelling about seeing names familiar to the local shipping industry within living memory. Fishers of Newry, Coppacks of Connah's Quay, and Gardeners of Lancaster are discussed, along with the vessels owned by the colliery itself.

The latter part of the story uses a blend of local knowledge and personal memoriesto offerwhat is hoped to be a lively description of the harbour and ships as places of work.The account tries to capture the work involved,particularly the hardship endured by the crews of the ships that carried coal away from the Point of Ayr wharf. Because it is possible to name many of the people involved, it may serve as a tribute to the men who sailed the ships, and to the families who supported them by sharing the disruption to their family life.

Regular exports ended in 1959, when the National Coal Board disposed of the last of their own ships, which had reached the end of her useful life. However, the story does not end untilfive years later with the last shipment in the October of 1963.

Having been a crew member of the vessel that took that last cargo to Peel, in the Isle of Man, I feel compelled to chronicle this brief history. I trust that those readers who have read my earlier works will forgive my repeating extracts from them. It is hoped that this booklet will be enjoyed by any who love industrial and maritime history, as well as those who know and love the vicinity. My fondest hope is that it mayinspire a new generation to delve deeper into the archival evidence and fill in the many remaining gaps. Our area tends to be overshadowed in the historical record by the bigger coalfields and the bigger seaports. For the benefit of any who care to rise to the challenge, my bibliography is appended.

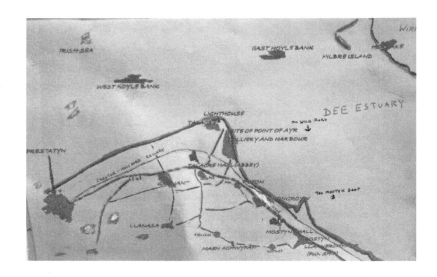

Above: Point of Ayr and Key points on coast and Dee Estuary,

Below: The Point of Ayr Colliery from Picton Courtesy Yvonne Robert

PART ONE

THE POINT IN EARLY TIMES

Long before the Point of Ayr harbour was used for the export of coal, the areawas a focus of activity. Geologists have told us how the forces of nature shaped it, bronze-age people occupied it, and the Romans had to control it to contain our iron-age ancestors. The Saxons controlled it for some sixty years, the Vikings visited it frequently, and the Normans and Welsh fought intense and bitter battles for its control. Part One offers a brief overview of these early years of the Point's history.

THE MAKING OF THE POINT

The deepest part of the Dee Estuary, the Wild Road, lies to the north of the Mostyn Bank, and was gouged out by the ice two million years ago, when the coastline was to the west of Ireland. As the ice melted, rising sea levels formed the Irish Sea and, about 10,000 years ago the sandbanks we now know as the Hoyle, the Middle Patch and the Salisbury Bank were islands of the Dee Delta. Over the next 2,000 years, the flowing and ebbing tides were forced between narrow gaps to carve deep channels and build a marshy coastline.

By BC3000, the coast was within today's tidal range, the high-water mark being close to the present low-water mark. Sea levels continued to rise, drowning the islands, and attenuating the force of the currents. The spring tides drove silt and boulders up from the marsh to create a sheltered coastline.

The spit we now know as the Point of Ayr was longer in the making, for the north and north-westerly winds that created the sand dunes at Talacre were countered by the prevailing southerlies, making for a long process, which was frequently reversed by extraordinarily high winds and tides. Some human encouragement helped, for much of the present coastline is the result of the enterprise of the Mostyns of Talacre Hall.

The Bronze Age people who mined the copper from the Orme's Head, around BC1600, would not have exported their product by sea, for boats were then only suitable for short fine weather trips. By BC500, however, sails were in use, and Caesar noted that the people of Western Europe built better sea–going vessels than those of the Mediterranean. Recent archaeological finds show that the people of Wales were competent shipbuilders.

The illustration below is based on an archaeological find near Tenby. In AD 300, Breton sailors could reach Ireland in two days.

Sailors entering the Dee estuary were helped by the beacon erected by the Romans at Whitford. to warn vessels bound for their great fortress at Chester of how close they were to the banks to their south. However, it may also have served as a guide to the approaches to creeks on the southern side.

Whether one of these was then close to the Point of Ayr, we do not know.At that time, the sea came up to the foot of Gwespyr Hill on today's coast road. It is possible that the Gwespyr stone used in the Prestatyn bath house was dragged down that ancient trackway, to be transported by sea to the Prestatyn gutter and up to where Melyd Avenue is today. Who knows? But there is much we do know about the development of the Point as a place of export.

A Celtic trading vessel, steered by two oars, based on an excavation near Tenby, dated to the first century AD.   W. Ken Davies 2020

Linguistic evidence suggests that the name *Point of Ayr* is derived from the Norse *Eyre*, and the name *Llinegr* could come from the Old Norse, *lin,* meaning flax. It is said that still-born babies were buried at Llwyn y Bedd; not a local custom, but one practiced by Irish descendants of settlers from Norway.

In AD 900, Aethelflaed a daughter of Alfred the Great, allowed Hiberno Norse people to settle on the Wirral, giving us names like Kirby and Helsby. Interactionbetween them and Welsh people wasinevitable, and probably intense.

There is no evidence of conflict, and most Norsemen were more interested in trade than booty. The people around Picton assimilated their influence, evidenced by the carvings on Maen Achwyfan, nearWhitford. The discovery of a Viking grave at Tanlan suggests the possibility of a Norse settlement. The high-water mark was then at the foot of the old cliff behind the pre-war houses, the beach offering shelter for the trading vessels.

Norse trading knarr.   *W. Ken Davies 2020*

The coast between Talacre and Mostyn would have remained busy throughout the middle-ages. Eleventh century Wales was ruled from Rhuddlan, and the Dee estuary was a cockpit of war for most of the period, as Anglo Saxon and Norman kings fought Welsh princes for controloverthe approaches to Chester. The Welsh had trading ships, incorporating Scandinavian features to develop the cog, which was frequently used for military purposes.

In 1044 Gruffydd ab Llewelyn defeated a Saxon fleet near Tenby, but on Christmas Eve in 1062,the Saxon Earl Harold Goodwinson, burned Gruffudd's fleet at Rhuddlan. Close links were developed with the Norsemen of Dublin, and Gruffydd ap Cynan's mother was a Norse princess. His son, Owain Gwynedd, in an alliance with his Norse kinsfolk, destroyedthe Norman castle at Prestatyn, annihilating the whole settlement.

Llywelyn Fawr traded with both England and Ireland, and, in 1212, King John sent a fleet to destroy his 'ships, galleys and boats.' His grandson, Llywelyn the Last encouraged Llanfaes merchants to trade with Liverpool, and used his ships in 1257 against Irish allies of Edward I. Trade between Wales and Dublin was well established by 1280, and a suburb of Dublin was called *Villa Wallensis,*meaningWelshtown.

During his castle building programme, Edward I had 30 ships carrying building materials and coal from the Dee to Conway, Beaumaris, and Caernarfon. With few quays, ships loaded and discharged their cargoes aground at low water. The creeks at Flint, Bagillt, Greenfield, Llannerch y Mor, Mostyn, and Llinegr were all convenient places for grounding ships to load from pack horses, mules or carts. During 1295, 2,428 tons of coal left the Dee for Beaumaris. In 1327, Edward III's troops probably embarked for Ireland from the estuary. Whilst the Black Death and plague had acceleratedadvancement in ship architecture, ships, were usually of forty tons or less. Few exceeded 100 tons; a 200 tonner was noted in 1325 as 'a big ship.'

Gruffydd ap Llywelyn's fleet afire at Rhuddlan in 1062.W.Ken Davies 2021

In 1400 Owain Glyndwr, supported by the notables of Tegeingl, took control of much of Wales. The Wirral was also in rebellion against HenryIVand supplied the Welsh with grain. Picton sailors would have ferried corn across the estuary for the nobles living at Nant Hall, and Golden Grove, their precious cargoes being off-loaded on the shores near the Point of Ayr.

PART TWO

THE RISE OF KING COAL

The Tudor dynasty ended over a thousand years of conflict for our ancestors from the Point of Ayr area. Every forty years or so, from AD 410, when the Romans left, until 1485, the people of Llinegr and Picton were called to arms to defend their territoryor, sometimes, to retrieve it from their enemies. The Tudor accession ended all that. A long period of peace ensued, and the next 200 years saw the rise of the coal export trade from around the Point of Ayr. Part Two deals briefly with this period, discussing the ships and sea-captains of Picton and Llinegr who developed the trade.

Howel ap Tudur of Mostyn had been a strong supporter of Glyndwr. Later in the century, his son in law, Ieuan Fychan, fought with the Lancastrians in the Wars of the Roses. Their claimant to the throne was Henry Tudor, the son of Owen Tudor, who had married the widow of King Henry V of England.

Ieuan FychanhidJasper, from his Yorkist enemies in Mostyn Hall. He escaped to Britanny from Picton Pool, which is believed to have been the origin of the Point of Ayr Harbour. Jasper had walked there from Mostyn disguised as a peasant carrying a bale of pease. His nephew Henry, also escaped by the same route when Ieuan's grandson, Richard ap Howel of Mostyn had hidden him from the Yorkists.

Following the Conquest of Edward I, the only named owners of Chester ships were Normans, but during the later Mediaeval period a small number of English merchants appear as owners. The first mention of a Welsh owner is by Elis Gruffydd, the noted Tudor historian from Gronant, who tells us that the vessel which saved Jasper Tudor,Henry Tudor's uncle, was owned by a gentleman of Whitford. Welsh seafarers were favoured under the Tudors, andmanyPicton and Llinegr gentlemen owned ships during the sixteenth century.

The Dee had been silting gradually since Roman times, and the process accelerated rapidly after the building of the Dee Mills in 1320. By1445 no merchant ship could get within twelve miles of Chester. Some action was taken to prevent silting in 1499, but by 1550 Mostyn was inaccessible, and Flint could harbour only fishing boats. This may have advantaged the ship-owners of Llinegr and Picton.

Tudor Trader of Carrickfergus   W.Ken Davies 2020

Possible image of a Tudor Period Picton Collier W.Ken Davies

19

When Henry VIII's shipbuilding program depleted timber stocks, it became profitable to mine coal. Early exports were small, and even bigger ships carried only ten chaldrons, just twenty tons. In 1565/1566, thirteen shipments to Dublin totalled 159 tons. Dublin took 95% of Flintshire's output of coal, from Picton Pool and the Welsh Lake, whichcould receive ships up to 100 tons, although vessels were generally much smaller. The trading season was short, from early spring to late autumn, and adverse winds could mean a vessel made only one or two trips in a year. In 1593 it took twelve ships thirty-five trips to move eighty-nine chaldrons, around 130 tons.

The population grew, and a major house-building program in the reign of Elizabeth I used up more forestry. Iron was required for cannon, and landowners were encouraged to exploit their coal reserves to replace charcoal in smelting iron and lead. Both Mostyn families were leaders in the search for coal under their land.

Mostyn and Llanasa Captains John Vaughan, Edmund ap Harry, David ap John, and William Davies frequently turn up in the records, commanding the *George,* the *Kathryn Thorneton,* the *Katrina,* the *Margaret,* the *Marie Grace,* the *Patrick,* the *Marie,* the *Peter,* the *MaryWalsyngham, Barbor,* the *Margaret Goodman,* and the*Kathryn Goodman.*

Bigger ships were developed during the century, but despite some deep-water anchorages, the shallow waters of the creeks of the Dee estuary meant that Picton and Mostyn ships remained small. The *Peter* is quoted at thirty tons, and the *Kathryn Goodman* at twenty-eight.

Trade continued under the Stuarts, when John Speed's map of 1611 showed very little change in the coastline. Dublin's population grew from 26,000 in 1611 to 40,000 in 1652, reaching 60,000 in 1680. The shipmasters were gentleman farmers as well as seafarers, making voyages as the demand arose. In 1607 a William Jones was master of the tiny *Mary William* of ten tons, and in 1609 well over 1000 tons left the Dee. By 1610 the upper reaches of the river were so badly silted that Heswall and Picton were the main ports.

Many vessels belonged to Picton, including the *Mary*, the *Katherine*, the *Angel*, the *Goodhope*, the *Peter,* and the *Susan,* all engaged in the export of coal. Edward Gregory of Llinegr, surely an ancestor of a Ffynnongroyw family which disappeared only in the nineteen-sixties, was master of a vessel called the *Cat* in 1612, the *Elizabeth,* and the *Janet* between 1614 and 1623. In 1630 Thomas Griffith was master of the *Mary*, of sixteen tons, and that decade saw homeward cargoes of agricultural produce commence.

The records for the next decades reveal numerous local shipmasters. In 1632 Griffith ab Evan was captain of the twelve tons *Ann of Picton.* 1634 saw Edward Griffith in charge of the *May* (twenty-six tons) and John Owen, master of the *Mary* of Picton, also of twenty-six tons. In 1639 Henry Jones was master of a bigger *Ann of Picton* being of twenty-four tons. Thomas Williams had the *Delight* of sixteen tons, and Hugh Jones the eighteen tons *Mary.*

William Gregory was master of the exotically named *Seville Orange* and the *Delight*, both of Picton in 1639 and 1641 respectively. Captain Hugh Jones commanded both the *Susan* and the *Angel* of Picton, whilst the *Good Hope* and the *Peter* of Picton sailed under Captain John Owen.

In 1633 there was a proposal to build a lighthouse at the Point of Ayr, but over a century was to pass before anything was done. Ships increased in size; those of the late Tudor period had averaged only nine tons, but in 1638 John Owen's *Maudlin* was of thirty-two tons, and the following year Bartholomew Morgan's *Katherine* was of twenty-six tons. In 1641 Thomas Lewis's *Susan* wasofthirty-six tons. Hugh Jones' *AngelofPicton*, John Owen's *Godspeed* and *Goodhope*, and Griffith Powell's *Peter* were probably of similar size.

Trade was brisk, and during 1639 over 5000 tons was exported from the Dee. The *Delight* made thirteen coastwise sailings during the year, at a time when vessels often only managed one or two trips a year.

In 1642 the Civil War broke out, and Picton people saw the Parliamentary Pinnace *Charity*, under Captain Danske, leading three ships around the Point of Ayr to blockade the estuary. By August many more parliamentary ships were riding at Point of Ayr. Picton men manned the vessels running the parliamentary blockade, and many vessels laden with coal and provisions were stopped. In the November of 1643, four of the king's ships disembarked troops at Mostyn, but the war was already as good as won by Cromwell's Ironsides.

Oliver Cromwell, the Protector of the new Commonwealth exacted stringent payment from those who supported the king.Both Mostyn families were treated harshly, beig stripped of land. Colonel Sir Roger Mostyn lost his home and had to live at Plas Ucha, a farm which still exist, near Tremostyn.

During the Cromwellian Commonwealth (1642 to 1660), production of coal was seriously reduced. Some was mined at y Gefron in Picton, but people endured hard times. Only two entries were made in the shipping records in1658, with Captain Evan Jones of the *Blessing*, and John Browne, captain of the *Lathdrum* of twenty tons. We know that ships were berthing at the Point of Ayr during these times, for in 1655, William Griffith, a mariner from Picton, was going to his ship at The Point of Ayr, when he claimed to have been bewitched. He had been imbibing at the tavern which became Tanlan Farm.

The English painter, William Turner, was fascinated by Flint Castle and the stretch of esturial shore. The first of Edward I's castles, it was the scene of Edward IV's victorious speech as portrayed by Shakespeare. Cromwell destroyed the castle, and Turner captures its forlornness.

23

Things improved intermittently after the monarchy was restored under Charles II.   Mostyn Hall was restored to the family, and there were small workings at Glasdir, Penyffordd, Glanrafon, and the Felin Blwm Ravine. There are notes of coal being raised at the Glasdir to be delivered to Talacre.

The export trade increased rapidly after 1660, and Dublin was receiving 95% of all Flintshire coal. However, by 1665 the approaches to Mostyn were seriously hampered by the dumping of ballast in the channel from the Wild Road, with only two or three fathoms of water compared to between six and eight off the Point of Ayr. Thus, it was the Point of Ayr that benefited when, at the end of the 1660s, a new fleet of colliers was built to meet demand in Dublin. Exports must have been given precedence over domestic needs, for as late as 1677 some Picton people had to go to Mostyn to buy coal.

Vessels were getting bigger, for war and plague had led to a general reduction in the size of the workforce, whilst demand was still rising. By 1672 the average vessel was over forty-five tons, and in 1682, the average cargo was fortychaldrons, almost eighty tons. By the end of the century few cargo vessels carried less than fifty tons, and ships were also more efficient. Before 1640, a crew of six was not unusual in a thirty-ton coaster. By 1680 average crews numbered a man for every twenty-eight tons, and the sloop had become the most popular coastal trader.

Roger Browne of Bryn Llinegre (sic) was master of the thirty-two tons *Hopewell* between 1666 and 1693, and John Browne, was master of the *Ann*. The family had been in Dee shipping since Elizabethan times, serving Dublin's growing population which had reached 60,000 by 1680.

These were wealthy men, either owning or having significant shares in the vessels. Frequently referred to as gentlemen, they had personal fortunes comparable with those of minor gentry like the Pennants. Lawrence Salthouse (alias Salters) of Llinegr, master of the *Satisfaction* in 1666, lived in a nine chambered house, and owned goods and chattels worth £294 14s and 8d. His son, Robert, was master of the seventy-four tons *Patience* in 1684.

Seventeenth Century trading sloop   *W. Ken Davies 2021*

In November1688, The Roman Catholic King James II was deposed and his protestant daughter, Mary was installed as joint monarch with her Dutch husband, King William III of Orange.

The TalacreMostyns seem to have worked to improve access to the Point, for achart, of which a fragment is shown overleaf, was presented to King William III. It shows an interesting profile of the Point of Ayre (sic.) in the late seventeenth Century.

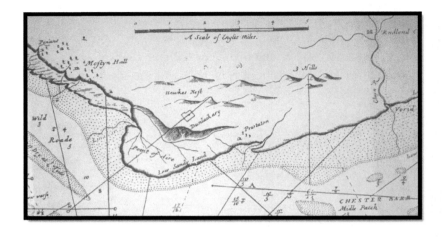

Extract from a chart presented to King William III 1688-1702
Courtesy Paul Parry

The marshy headland hooks eastward from Talacre almost to Llinegr, the entrance to the harbour being from that end. The survey found ten fathoms of water in the Wild Road, and it is worthy of note that a bearing directly onto Talacre Hall is shown. The king's interest would bedue to the possibility that Sir Pyers Mostyn, being a Catholic, posed a threat to the control of the approaches to Chester. There was also a strong Jesuit presence at Holywell nearby, and King William III and Queen Mary would have been sensitive to the potential dangers, as they struggled to secure the Protestant succession.

PART THREE
THE MODERN HARBOUR
IS DEVELOPED

Throughout the Tudor and Stuart periods coal had been exported without the benefit of many quays or jetties. Mostyn had a rudimentary quay near the pits, but it was frequently inaccessible. Ships were loaded on the ground from pack-horses or mules at low water, or transhipped from small boats when afloat. Part Three starts with the turbulent years of the eighteenth century, with its lawlessness and disorder. It goes on to discuss the bold capital developments spearheaded by the Mostyns of Talacre. Land is reclaimed from the sea, the tides of the estuary are tamed, and a modern harbour is built. Shipbuilding is established locally, and the stage is set for the coming of the railway. The days of the Point of Ayr Colliery, and even more ambitious plans appear on the horizon, only to be dashed by fruitless litigation.

THE EIGHTEENTH CENTURY

In 1700, Sir Pyers Mostyn of Talacre entered into an agreement with a landowner called Margaret Griffiths of Gyrne, allowing him to mine coal and transport it to the sea for export. Although the agreement laid the foundations for the larger scale Picton Collieries, the fortunes of the Point of Ayr as a harbour declined. The 6,000 or so tons of coal exported in 1701 shrank to just a couple of hundred by 1742, despite the growth of Dublin's population from 10,000 in 1640 to 130,000 by 1740.

A series of violent high tides during the last decade of the seventeenth century accelerated the silting of the estuary between Holywell Brook and the Point of Ayr, and silting continued, into the eighteenth century. By 1710, in the reign of Queen Anne, vessels above sixty tons could not access the harbour. During that year only 4,000 tons of coal was exported from the whole of Flintshire. Much trade was lost to Cumberland because of the small size of the Dee vessels and fewer homeward cargoes of agricultural produce from Ireland.

Trade did pick up, and 1735 saw almost 10,000 tons exported. It is not clear from whence these shipments went, for the sketch opposite suggests that both Mostyn and the Point of Ayr were completely silted over. The broad spit shown in the 1690 chart seems to have been completely obliterated, the sand being washed into the old harbour. The only outlet may have been from the outflow of the Holywell Brook at Greenfield.

It was alsoa dangerous time to be a sailor. Local people frequently plundered the wrecks of vessels driven ashore in stormy weather, and between 1757 and the end of the century fifteen vessels were wrecked on the coast of the Parish of

Llanasa. The seaman also ran the risk of being impressed into the Navy.

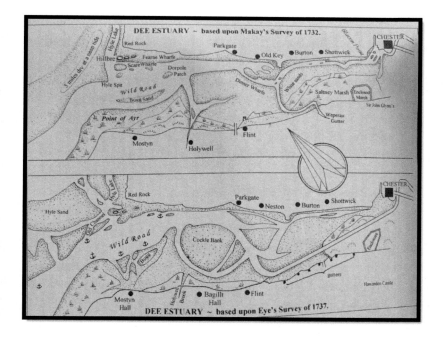

The sailors of the Dee were very active in the smuggling trade, with armed smuggling ships and revenue cutters battling for control. Smuggling was considered respectable by the localpeople, as it furnished many luxuries otherwise denied them by high duties. One vessel built at Rhuddlan is listed as being ordered specially 'for the smuggling trade'.

Picton ships like the *Speedwell*, *Morning Star*, and *Charming Molly* were often involved, and vessels freighting coal from the Point of Ayr up-rivertrans-shipped illicit goods. The Isle of Man, beyond the reach of English Law, was a gigantic clearing house for smuggled goods. On one occasion a great deal of wine was seized from the great barn at Talacre and impounded at the Lletty Inn at Glan-y-Don, only to be 'liberated' by the locals. When the Isle of Man was annexed by the Crown smuggling became more violent, and River Dee mariners were prominent in establishing a new base at Rush, a fishing port near Dublin.

Things did not immediately improve for the Point when the Dee was canalized between Flint and Chester in 1737. The River Dee Company was established in 1740 to maintain the navigation of the channel to Chester, and 1753 saw the Dee Navigation Act passed. However, the authority of the Dee Company did not extend beyond Llinegr, and the stone placed in 1790 to mark that limit can still be seen.

By 1755, around 5000 tons were exported from the estuary. The population of Dublin reached 130,000 by 1750, and in 1763, around 10,000 tons left the Dee. However, Drogheda, Dundalk, Strangford, and the Isle of Man were taking most Flintshire coal, with small quantities going to Newfoundland, Charlestown, Carolina, NewYork and Barbados. By 1770, 15000 tons were exported.

It can be seen from the sketch on page 30 that the New Dee Cut brought the channel over to the Welsh side, with the suggestion of some possibility of high-wateraccess to Mostyn and the Point of Ayr. The drainage of the Trelogan mines into Nant y Garth had improved the flow to the harbour so, given the accessibility ofPicton coal, and the interest of the Mostyn Family at Talacre Hall, it seems likely that the Point of Ayr exported its fair share of this tonnage.

The Napoleonic Wars caused serious food shortages, with rioting all over Flintshireto prevent corn exports from the ports. Local nobles reclaimed marshland for food production and, in 1812 Sir Piers Mostyn reclaimed the coastal marsh between Gronant and Llinegr from the sea.The sand dunes were reinforced, and the cob from Talacre to Ffynnongroyw constructed.

The harbour was developed at the end of the gutter created in 1794, with a granary and buildings built on the south side, to create the coastal configuration seen below.

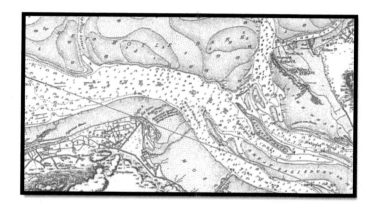

From nineteenth century hydrographic chart Courtesy Paul Parry

By 1838 John Dawson had a shipyard near the harbour, and in 1839 the most recent channelwas cut, running roughly east to west from the Wild Road.On 2nd December of that year, John Hargreaves Douglas of Gyrn agreed to permit Irish and London merchants to mine coal and ironstone under lands at Picton, Gwespyr and Axton for a term of thirty-one years. Crockford's tramwaywas constructed the following year, running from Glanrafon via Picton Pits, down the incline known as the Brake, and on to the harbour.

A shipyard at Sluice built flats and schooners between sixty and 150 tons, as well as one schooner of 253 tons, a sizeable vessel at that time. An active shipyard in Ffynnongroyw itself used the pool that existed between the site of the present Tanrhiw and Uwchlyn cottages, which were later converted from its workshops. The area was known as the township of Trewaelod, 'the bottom, or lower town.'

In 1843 two boreholes were sunk to the south of the Talacre Cob and, in 1846, 115 acres between Mostyn and Talacre became the responsibility of the River Dee Company.A composite map,produced in 1954 by Hawson,shows all developments to the harbour between 1839 and 1952. It dates a revetment wall protecting the north-east side of the harbour to 1847, clearly part of the Chester-Holyhead Railway Project. The same project created the railway embankment from Mostyn westward which gave us today's coastline.

In 1865, another three boreholes proved the coalfield extended under the estuary, and Sir Pyers Mostyn obtained an act of parliament permitting the construction of a harbour at the Point of Ayr. In 1866 the Prestatyn Colliery Company was formed, with ambitious plans, including a pier from the colliery to the Wild Road at the low water mark, and a breakwater on the Salisbury Bank. A dispute over mineral ownership between Sir John Hanmer and Sir Pyers Mostyn followed. The litigation dragged on for several years and the company went bankrupt.

PART FOUR
THE POINT OF AYR COLLIERY

The heyday of the Point of Ayr as a coal exporting port begins in 1884, when disaster strikes Mostyn, just two miles to the south. Differences are buried, and a combination of dire need and initiative forges the incentive for interested parties to rise to the challengeandcreate the new colliery, which commences production in 1890. Part Three explores this period, with the development of bigger and better ships, the trades they served, and the crews who sailed them.

THE MODERN POINT IS BORN

Disaster struck Mostyn on the22nd July 1884, when the pits were flooded beyond salvation by sea water, and the Point project was hastily resurrected.

The Point of Ayr Collieries Ltd. was formed, chaired by Charles Batters, with a manager called Gilderoy. A cob was built around the whole area to secure the pit from the sea. The derelict shaft was dewatered and completed, and a second shaft was sunk. Extraction from the Five Yard seam commenced in 1890, and a tramway was constructed to take coal to the weighbridge at the main road.

Batters immediately exploited the potential for export to the ready market for the excellent house-coal in Ireland, the Isle of Man and other ports around the British coast, using a stone berth to the north of the quay now preserved on the coastal path. On census night in April 1891, there were five vessels alongside at the Point of Ayr. Four were the sailing flats *Odessa, Nina, Zoar and William &Alice.*Thesloop-rigged Mersey flat had been developed during the previous century, the average size increasing steadily from fifty-seven to seventy-six tons. Duringthe nineteenth century, carrying around 100 tons, and handled by two men, it was the most popular vessel in Liverpool Bay.

The registered owner of the *Odessa, Nina,* and *Zoar* was Mr Thomas Robinson of 20,Water Street, Liverpool. During the six-month period, the Odessa made sixteen voyages from the Point to other creeks on the estuary, probably maintaining supplies of coal to the Mostyn Ironworks. Her master was twenty-eight-year-old Frank Pierce of Flint, his mate being sixteen years old John Bithel of the same town.

Mersey flat under sail W. Ken Davies 2020

The master of the *Nina* was JohnBithel's father, Stephen. With his mate, thirty-seven years old Thomas Jones, also of Flint, Captain Bithel had completed fifteen voyages between the Dee and Mersey during the six months, the Point being her usual loading port. Thomas Jones paid off at the end of June to be replaced by eighteen years old George Frances Peers of the same town.

The *Zoar* had spent the half year trading both within the estuary and with Liverpool, manned by twenty-three years old Captain John Davies of Bagillt, and his mate, nineteen years old

Robert John Jones of the same town, who had replaced twenty years old Robert Conway of Flint the previous year.

The sailing flat *William and Alice* was owned by William Heaps of Everton Valley, Liverpool. Under Captain Henry Barron of Burscough, near Southport, she loaded for Beaumaris. The *William and Alice* had had two mates during the six months, being CaptainBarron's sons, twenty years old John and eighteen years old Henry. It was her only visit to the Point during the six months, other ports visited being Flint, Greenfield, Liverpool, Widnes, and Port Dinorwic.

The *Pilgrim*, carrying around 140 tons, was owned by Richard Atherton of Aintree. Captain Walter Hulse of Winsford, with his mate, twenty-three-year-old Joseph Jones of Greenfield, traded regularly between the Point, Greenfield, Rhyl, and Liverpool,completing twenty-seven voyages in six months.

For all its efficiency, the days of the Mersey flat as a seagoing vessel were drawing to a close, due to the development of the coasting schooner. The schooner was developed during the late seventeenth century. It was originally a vessel with fine lines, built for speed, andfor this reason one was used to carry Nelson's body, pickled in brandy, home from Trafalgar. It could originally be square rigged, but later fore-and aft sails only were favoured, as developed by the Americans to overcome labour shortages during the nineteenth century.

The schooner was brought to its ultimate perfection by Porthmadog shipbuilders, who built them to transport slates across the Atlantic. They combined square and fore-and-aft rigs to produce the topsail schooner, which soon dominated the coastal trade. Two masted vessels were easily handled by two men and a boy, who was usually the cook. Bigger schooners with three masts carried 180 tons and needed only two more men.

During the early years of the century, production at the colliery dropped to around 18,979 tons. In 1907, the tramway to the screens and the sidings at Talacre was built, and the following year production reached 41,060. By 1910, when George V was crowned, around nine ships visited the jetty each week. That year saw 457 vessels carry 35,554 tons of Point coal away.

Topsail schooners slowly ousted the Mersey Flat. W.Ken Davies 2019

The sailing flats were being ousted by schooners and the occasional steamer, and on census night on April 1st 1901, the only two flats at the Wharf, were the *Confidence* of Preston, and the *Dalton* of Chester, carrying around 100 tons each.

Nine vessels in all were alongside, including two steamers. The *Emily* of Chester would have loaded about 180 tons, and the *Exchange* of Liverpool perhaps as much as 240. She was built of iron at Amlwch in 1884 by William Thomas and Sons. She was owned by William Thomas Jnr.,who operated out of Liverpool. Later that year she was acquired by the Manchester, Liverpool and North Wales Steamship Company Ltd., but in 1917 was sunk by gunfire by the German submarine UB 39 off the French Coast.

The steamship Exchange, which loaded at the Point in 1901, was built during the last decade of the 19th Century.   *W. Ken Davies 2020*

The schooners *Claggan*and*Ellis Park* of Barrow, would have loaded around 250 tons between them, whilst the Lancaster schooner *Mary Goldsworthy* might have taken another hundred. Also at thewharf were two Cardigan ketches, the *Cymric* and *Enid,* carrying perhaps fifty tons each. The ketch was more lightly rigged than the schooner, carrying no topsails. The mainsail was on the foremast with a spanker on a short mizzen mast ahead of the steering gear.

The small schooners *Wyre* of Fleetwood, and *Jubilee* of Preston were anchored off the Point.Between them they would have taken around another 200 tons or so, making about 1200 tons.

Ten years later, on census night in 1911, there were three steamers and two flats on the wharf. The Liverpool flats, *Ellen*and *Providence*, would carry around 100 and 150 tons respectively. The Glasgow steamer *Loch Doon*, a small iron-built steamer of the previous century, would have taken away 150 tons.

The modern steel steamers *Carlingford* of Dundalk, and *Clwyd* of Liverpool were models of the future. Carrying around 250 tons each, ships like them would becameubiquitous around the Irish Sea and Bristol Channel for over half a century.

The steamer Clwyd R & D Jones, Liverpool   *W. Ken Davies 2020*

Fishers of Newry

Local people referred to all the vessels that visited regularly as 'Point boats.' Many were chartered, but others, belonged to Irish merchants who purchased Point coal, including Joseph Fisher of Newry. The steamer *Upas* belonged to himand has an interesting but tragic connection with the village of Ffynnongroyw.

The steamship Upas   *Courtesy Captain B. Luke*

She was a large version of the typical three masted vessel of the period. Being almost 170 feet long, it is unlikely that she ever visited the Point, but her master, Captain William McFerran certainly had, for on August 5th 1907, he married, Sarah Jane Evans of Ffynnongroyw. They lived on the fashionable Bridge Street, Newry, home to several master mariners.

On March 18th 1915, fate treated the family cruelly. The *Upas*' cargo shifted in a south easterly gale off Birr Point on the coast of Northern Ireland. In a howling blizzard, the vessel did not stand a chance. Two of the nine men aboard were saved, but their shipmates suffered terribly before dying. Captain McFerran went down with his ship and, according to eyewitnesses ashore, behaved admirably. In those days, such an event was a catastrophe for a family. Captain and Mrs McFerran's little daughter, Jean, joined a Ffynnongroyw family, where she grew up to become Mrs. Luke, a respected member of the community.

Captain and Mrs McFerran   Courtesy Captain B. Luke

41

Coppacks of Connah's Quay

The resourceful Coppack Brothers of Connah's Quay developed a fruitful relationship with the colliery. They skillfully supplied suitable tonnage to transport slack from the Point to Price's Candle factory at Bromborough. In 1928 they acquired the auxiliary sailing vessel *Santa Rosa,* which carried 170/180tons on a draught of nine feet. In 1934 she went afire in the Wild Roads and was lost, to be replaced by the *Trevor,*built in Northwich by Yarwoods for Henry Seddon of Liverpool.

After thirteen years' service, she was sold to the Isle of Man and then to Garston. She then spent just two years with south Wales owners before Coppacks bought her to do the Bromborough run for the last three years of her life. Too heavily draughted for the Point, she would often be loaded down by the head, and pushed down the gutter with her starboard bilge against the mud. Her bow plates wereworn thin by the experience. Being uneconomical to repair, she was broken up on Tranmere beach.

Thesteamer Trevor.   *W..Ken Davies, 2019*

The *Trevor*'s successor was possibly the best loved visitor to the Point,being the wooden auxiliary sailing vessel *Bolham*. Built at Rye in 1913 as the *Sarah Colebrooke*, she was taken by the Admiralty in 1917 and renamed *HMS Bolham*. She became a Q-ship during the First World Warand sank a U-boat.

Often under sail, she must have awakened the family's consciousness of their beginnings, when Captain John Coppack, master and owner of sailing vessels, set up his brokerage in his front room at Connah's Quay.

The acquisition of the *Bolham*, however, was no romantic exercise. Carrying 250 tons on a draught of eight feet, she had six owners before Coppacks bought her in 1938. She was ideal for the Point of Ayr – Bromborough run, carrying slack to Price's candle factory. Re-engined in 1943, she served them until 1958.

With the Bromborough run in mind, the brothers bought the motor vessel *Fleurita,*from the Summers steel producers at Shotton in 1945. She had been built in 1913 at Queensferry by I.J.Abdela and Mitchelland served Summers well for twenty-eight years. With her shallow draught, she too was ideal for the Bromboroughrun.In 1961her outdated Swedish Bolinder engine was replaced by a Crossley diesel. She was sold to Civil and Marine of London, only to sink with a cargo of sand and gravel two miles south-west of the Gunfleet Light whilst on passage from Felixtowe to London.Fortunately, no lives were lost.

Coppacks acquired another of Summers' motorships, the *Indorita* in 1946. Built at the same yard as the *Fleurita*, she too served Summers well. Although more often to be found general coasting under Coppacks, she frequently visited the Point of Ayr, and appears again in the final chapter of our story. Re-engined in 1958, she was broken up in Spain in 1971.

Above: The motor vessel Fleurita.   *Courtesy Rhiw photos*

Below: Artist's impression of a.s.v. Bolham under sail.   *W.Ken Davies 2019*

Above: A sadder view of the Bolham awaiting demolition at Connah's Quay Courtesy theCoppack Family.

Below: Coppacks' motor vessel Normanby Hall visited the Point of Ayr but once, as related in the final chapter.   *W. Ken Davies 2017*

Gardeners of Lancaster

Robert Gardener of Lancaster owned the *Maurita, River Loyne, Multistone, Mountcharles,* and *Calyx,* all of which visited the jetty quite frequently. During the Second World War, the steamer *Maurita,* with Captain Robert Hutton of Connah's Quay in command, was mined near Hilbre with the loss of all hands.

A previous master of the *Maurita,* the Cornishman, Captain Hugh Pyburn married Marian Williams of Picton, where he settled and raised his family. Hugh Pyburn and his brother, James, were both schooner veterans. Captain James Pyburn was master of Gardener's Calyx, a particularly attractive little motor coaster, built in Holland.

An interesting vessel, Gardener's motor ship,the*River Loyne* had been built by J.T. Eltringham & Co. Ltd. at Willington Quay-on-Tyne for the Admiralty. Originally intended to land troops at the Dardenelles during the First World War, she was not used until 1922, when she was rebuilt and lengthened at Connah's Quay. She retained her square bow, which could originally be droppedasa ramp for the troops to cross onto the beach.

The*River Loyne* was acquired By Gardener in 1925, to be successfully operated until the December of 1948, when she sank with all hands in a north-westerly gale off Puffin Island. Two local fishermen had taken a trip as a favour to Captain Carmichael, a jovial man who always had a small brown-and-white dog at his heels. It was a sad day in the Point of Ayr area. Both the*River Loyne* and the *Calyx* can be seen opposite.

The motor vessel River Loyne was lost with all hands in 1948
W.Ken Davies 2020

The motor vessel Calyx .Courtesy Rhiw Photos.

During the First World War, the colliery became a ship owner. The wartime loss of shipping was immense, and the firm saw it as advisable to have a ship available at their behest. By coincidence, one of the vesselsat the wharf on census night, 1911, the steamer *Clwyd*, seen on page 39became the colliery's first ship.

She had been built in1909 in South Shields by J.P. Reynoldson for Richard and David Jones, two Welsh brothers who operated a sizeable fleet of coastal and short-sea traders out of Liverpool. In 1916 she was bought by the colliery, only to be lost on 19th December 1917,when she sank after colliding with the large steamer *Paragon,*twelve miles north of the Skerries, off Anglesey. Captain John Jones of Bangor and his six crew were thirty-four hours in the lifeboat, before being rescued by a Fleetwoodtrawler and landed on the Isle of Man. The chief engineer, forty-seven years old William Owen Jones of YrFelinheli, had died of exposure.

The *Clwyd* had already been joined in the August of that year by the brand new steamship *Talacre,* built at Yarmouth for the company by Crabtree and Co. Ltd., and the *Clwyd* was replaced in 1922 by the steamer *Solway Firth.* She had been launched two years earlier by J. Cran and Somerville, Ltd. at Leith for the Newcastle based Border Shipping Companybut was not completed until the colliery acquired her.She was renamed *Point of Ayr*, and the photograph opposite shows her as she was when acquired by the company. There was no wheelhouse, the only protection on the bridge from wind and weather being the canvas dodger. As well as the usual foremast and derrick driven by a steam winch, she had a mast before the bridge carrying a derrick driven by a second steam winch. Some ten years later these were removed and the winch used as a replacement aboard the *Talacre.*

Above: the steamship Talacre:　　　　　　*Author's family Archive*
Below: The steamship Point of Ayr as in 1922　*Courtesy Rhiw Photos*

*With the wheelhouse fitted by the company, The Point of Ayr leaves
Liverpool's Gladstone Dry Dock.   Courtesy Gareth Edwards*

The *Tanlan*was built in 1914 for R & D Jones'as the*Elwy,* by
Charles Reynoldson and Company at South Shields. In 1917, she
was sold to Abraham Lazarus of London, who sold her to Claude
Langdon of Liverpool a year later. Belfast owners, William
Stewart and James Orr, acquired her in 1920, selling her to
Spillers the millers the following year. Called the *Wheatfeed,*
theyran her until 1933, when she was bought by the Colliery,who
also employed Mr. Waterson as shore superintendent.

The Tanlan alongside and at sea. Photo courtesy Paul Parry

W. Ken Davies 1998

Above: The Point of Ayr alongside at the Point. Courtesy Paul Parry

Below: The Talacre at sea, off Carmel Point in 1957
Author's family Archive

PART FIVE

WORK, TRADES AND MEN

Everything involving coaland its movement meanthardphysical work. The gruelling work of the men who cut the coal and moved it underground and up to the surface is well documented elsewhere. The hardships of working the harbour, loading the coal onto the ships, and moving it across the sea are not as well known. Seagoing is popularly regarded as an easy-going, romantic – even idyllic life. The truth is verydifferent, and Part Five offers a more down-to-earth description of these aspects of the coal industry.

The sailing vessels continued to be served by the tugboat, driven in 1901 by Hugh Griffiths of number three Denbigh Row. In the village, Stanmore House was home to the Point of Ayr harbourmaster, Captain Albert Carter, a Cornishman who established a well-known local family. Indeed, his great-grandson, Paul Parry has not only published a history of this interesting familybut has done invaluable work in gathering many elements of local historytogether. Captain Carter was followed by Richard Hughes of Ffynnongroyw.

An aerial view of the colliery and harbour, showing the coastline north-west from Ffynnongroyw   *Courtesy Paul Parry*

Everything to do with the export of coal involved hard work. The harbour had its problems. The dangers of the approaches to the estuary, the shallow waters, and the dependency on tides made the channel a tricky place to navigate. A boatman was employed to secure the ships' mooring ropes and, as the vessel approached the end of the channel, he sculled across the harbour to secure a line to the hook on the barrel-buoy shown in the picture below. The vessel, assisted by the tug-boat, was then hauled around through 180 degrees to point down channel when in her berth under the loading chute.

The gutter was marked with eleven perches, tall baulks of timber firmly embedded in the sand. When a vessel sailed at night they were lit by oil-lamps. These were placed at low water by the boatman, who, with a ladder on his shoulder, carried the heavy lamps on a purpose made belt around his waist. He was also responsible for maintaining the gutter. At low water, after opening the sluice-gates to scour the channel, he would inspect the waterway, dig out unwanted accumulations of sand, and lay bramble and hawthorn bushes to bind the walls of the bank.

A view of the harbour from the early 20th Century.

Author's Family Archive

The 1911 census names the boatman as Hermann Forsmann, a native of Finland, who lived in a hut near Point of Ayr House. Better known as Charlie the gutter-man, he was a member of the local lifeboat crew. He died in 1922 of pulmonary oedema. It said that he had collapsed in the gutter and suffered exposure. Charlie was succeeded by Edward Blythin of Lifeboat Cottages, another lifeboat-man and schooner veteran.

The tubs of coal were drawn by a horse straight from the pit-head, to the quayside. Two men would upend each tub into a chute which took the coal into the hold of the vessel alongside the jetty. This method prevailed until the mid-fifties when a crane was introduced to empty large boxes.The old system was punishing work, for the operatives were exposed to wind, weather and coal-dust. Yet, the job was often done by old or infirm ex-colliers. When the pit hooter blew for knocking off time, the horse would kick off the traces and bound off to the stables near the under-manager's house. Sometimes men and horse had to work late to finish loading a vessel to sail on the evening tide, and the horse would object strongly if not rewarded with tit-bits.

In later years, an awkward bend developed just clear of the jetty. As the gutter ran across the tideway, it was easy to ground on the northern bank when leaving on the ebb. The solution was to wait for low waterwhen the crew would attach a mooring line to a plank. The plank would be buried deeply in the sand on the southern bank. On the next tide, the ship could be hove back into the channel. Once afloat, the rope would be severed with a specially sharpened axe. The engineers would be rung for full speed ahead, and the vessel would carry on the voyage. There was no local pilot, so strangers frequently grounded if trying to make the harbor two late on the ebb. Sometimes they were neaped for several days.

This delightful photograph is of the ladies who staffed the colliery canteen, From left; Elsie Jones, Mary Mealor (nee Parry), Gladys Jones, Rhiannon Kenny (nee Jones) and Hilda Jones. By chance we have a unique shot of the Tanlan swinging to take the berth.

Courtesy Captain B. Luke

The Talacre, using the windlass to heave herself off the bank.

Author's family archive

PORTS, VOYAGES, AND THE CREWS' WORK

The main agents buying Point coal were across the Irish Sea. On the east coast of the Republic of Eire, they were based at Dundalk, Drogheda and Dublin, as well as the more southerly ports of Wexford. Waterford, and New Ross. There was also a trade with Cork and, before World War Two, many ports on the Atlantic seaboard. In Northern Ireland, the colliery supplied the power station at Newry, as well as merchants in Carrickfergus, Belfast and Derry. There was also an important trade with all the Manx ports.

The three nearest Irish discharging portsof Dublin, Drogheda and Dundalk are between 110 and 120 nautical miles from the Point of Ayr Lighthouse, and we can use Drogheda to help describe the work involved for the crews. For the sake of simplicity, we can imagine a ship loading at the Point on a Monday. This may have been following the rare luxury of a weekend alongside at the Point or, more usual and painful, arrival during the weekend, or the early hours of the morning. We can also imagine that she will sail at high water around 4.00 p.m., neatly between a spring and neap tide.

Whilst the ship was loading, the crew would be busy with ship's work, punctuated with a mile walk to Ffynnongroyw to buy victuals, usually from Blackwell's grocery store at the top of what is now Williams' Place. The dinner hour would be spent planning the return walk at the Farmer's Arms over a pint or two.

If the deck crew was lucky, loading might be completed in time to secure the ship for sea. This was hard work, heaving heavy hatch-boards up to cover the hold, and spreading two canvas covers which were firmly wedged home and secured with wires strops or steel locking bars. This was a particularly heavy job aboard the *Talacre*, as her long hatch-boards lay half-way

58

across the hatch onto fore-and-aft beams between the crossbeams. She also had high coamingsso the hatch-boards had to be lifted higher.

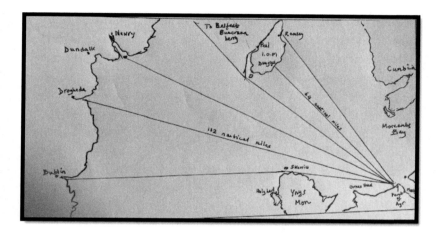

Courses and distances between the Point of Ayr Lighthouse and the ports on the east coast of Ireland and the Isle of Man (Scale approximate).W.Ken Davies

With cutting tides, it was necessary to ensure the vessel floated at high water.The forward part of the hatch was left open, with ten or twenty tons left on the quay to trim her by the head, raising the stern clear of the ground. Once clear of the gutter, the ship could be trimmed to the captain's liking with the tanks.

Meanwhile, the engineers and firemen would have been busy taking bunkers, the coal that would fire the boiler, trimming it in the space below. They would also raise the steam ready for sailing. After leaving, and following a day's work, which may have begun when berthing at around 3.30 that morning, they would work watch-and-watch, four hours on and four hours off,through the night. At the end of each watch, the fireman and a sailor would wind up the ashes from the stoke-hold in five-hundred-weight bags, to be emptied overboard from the lee side.

On arrival 'on the other side,' in time to start discharging at eight a.m. on Tuesday morning, the hard work carried on. Before discharging, the deck crew 'stripped her,' removing the heavy tarpaulins, perhaps sodden with sea from a rough passage. After stacking the hatch-boards on deck, the cross beams would be taken out and stowed on deck. These were girders, some sixteen feet long by four feet deep, slotted into each side of the hatchway. They served the dual function of giving the vessel transverse strength when at seaand supporting the hatch-boards and tarpaulins that kept her from filling up with water and sinking. The photograph opposite shows the deck crew of the Point of Ayr unshipping or shipping the beams with the derrick driven by the ship's winch.

The cargo was usually discharged with that same derrick and winch, so the engine room and stokehold men spent their day maintaining steam. The Irish coal heavers were usually on piece-work and worked hard and quickly, shoveling the coal into tubs or skips to be winched out of the hold and across onto the quay, using a system known as a 'swinging derrick.' Irish winch drivers were notoriously ruthless in their demands for steam, keeping the firemen and engineers busy.

Discharging would be completed during the afternoon, and the deck crew would be hard put to secure the vessel for sea, replacing the beams, throwing up the hatch-boards, spreading the tarpaulins, and securing them with wedges. The 'down-below' men raised steam again, ready for another night of watch-and-watch. The coasting sailor lost a lot of sleep.

If there was another load waiting at the Point, and the neaping tides allowed sufficient water, she would get there ready to load on Wednesday to sail on the tide at around 6.00 p.m.

Deck crew shipping beams   *Photo from author's family archive*

Weather permitting, she could be unloading again on Thursday. By Friday, small tides may not allow her access to the Point. Were the gods to be smiling, she might go to Mostyn, a deeper berth, and enjoy a night or two at home, moving to the Point on Sunday morning's tide to load on Monday.

The gods seldom smiled so benignly, and the vessel would be sent to load road-stone at one of the quarry jetties in Caernarfon Bay. She would reach there to load on the early morning tide, an onerous task requiring all hands. The watch below would lose most of their beauty sleep and be up most of the night. They would arrive at Liverpool's Carriers Dock on Thursday afternoon, and discharge on Friday. If there was a vacant berth at Mostyn, she mightgo there to wait for the Sunday tide at around 10 a.m or 10.30 p.m and move to the Point ready to load on Monday morning.

Newry: A special case.

The Newry run posed problems of its own. From the Point it is almost 109 miles to the difficult entrance to Carlingford Lough. The lough cannot be accessed on an ebb tide, which can run up to five knots off Greenore Point. With a further six miles to the Newry Canal, at nine knots a ship cannot catch the following tide and would have to lie at anchor for several hours, losing half a day's discharging time.

The answer was to schedule voyages to make the steamer *Point of Ayr* available for the Newry cargoes. Her ingenious Chief Engineer, Charles Dennis of Holywell, had worked on her sizeable engine to increase her speed from a grudging nine knots to a lively ten. Even at an economical speed of 9.5 she could scrape into Newry on the morning tide, ready to discharge and leave that evening. Good for the company, but harsh on her crew, a trip to the quarries and Liverpool would make for a hard week.

The extra turn of speed was also an advantage on the longer runs north to Belfast, Derry, and Buncrana, or south to Wexford, Waterford, New Ross, Cork and beyond to small ports on the Irish Atlantic seaboard. From the Point to Waterford is around 183 nautical miles, and that extra knot took as much as two hours off sailing time if time was short. The *Point of Ayr* also had more bunker-space than the others, another saving with no need to buy bunkers for the return trip.

The above account assumes fine weather at a particular point in the lunar tidal cycle. Adverse winds were very frequent in winter,and disrupted schedules severely. To miss a late afternoon tide at the Point would mean the loss of a precious night at home. It could also mean berthing in the early hours of the following morning, work all day whilst loading, only to leave o n the evening tide to work watch-and-watch all night.

The following daycould easily see the cargo discharged in time for the vessel to sail that evening. The crew would have to spend the day attending to the necessary work of the vessel, and would face yet another night of watch-and-watch. The crews led a harsh and uncertain life, and we may well ask why men tolerated such a grim way of earning a living. The discussion of the crews in the following section throwsa little light on this question.

By contrast, the Isle of Man run could be idyllic. Leaving on that Monday afternoon tide, at an economical nine knots, arrival at Douglas Pier, just 68 nautical miles away, would be at around 11.p.m. The vessel would enter the harbour and berth at around 5.00 am on Tuesday. Having discharged, she would leave on the evening's tide. Should she berth and load on Wednesday, she would probably beneaped until Sunday morning,the crew gaining four nights at home.

The firm would be more likely to arrange a road-stone cargo instead, to be discharged at Carriers Dock, Liverpool on Thursday. If a berth could be found, she may lay in Liverpool until Sunday, or else move to Mostyn on the Saturday evening's tide in time for a pint or two in the Hotel which is now a nursing home. Even on the comparatively benign Isle of Man run, the crew's leisure time depended very much on the mood of the gods.

THE MEN WHO SAILED THE SHIPS

Captain Charles Williams was master of the steamship *Talacre* for most of her long life. A veteran of both schooners and the Royal Navy, Captain Williams came from Connah's Quay, butlived at Hazeldene inTanlan. He was well known in the community. He succeeded Captain Louis Carter, a veteran of the Dardanelles, where he had been wounded.

Captain Charles Williams   *Courtesy Angela Roberts*

Captain James Thomas, a native of Amlwch, was the last master of the *Point of Ayr*. He too settled in Tanlan, later moving to Prestatyn. The photograph below shows him at the helm of a subsequent command, a hyper-modern container carrier, the motor vessel *Irishgate*. He was the nephew of the first master of the Point of Ayr, Captain Richard Evans, who was noted for his indifference to bad weather. It is really a shame that we do not have a photograph of him.

Captain James Thomas   *Photo courtesy Lisa Jones.*

The master of the *Point of Ayr* between Captain Evans and and Captain Thomas, was Captain David Hutton, another schooner veteran from Connah's Quay. His brother, Captain Robert Hutton, was master of Gardener's *Maurita* when she was lost with all hands during World War Two.

Captain Lamb, master of the *Tanlan*, was a native of Bath. He had been a deep sea master with the Branch Line, trading to the Mediterranean and Black Sea. Becoming a coasting sailor during the lean times of the hungry thirties, he had quite simply taken to the life He was master of the *Tanlan* with several earlier owners, under the names of *Elwy* and *Wheatfeed*.

Another deep sea captain who was relief master was Captain Downing who came to the Point of Ayr as mate from the Bibby line, trading to the far east. Another relief master was the Ffynnongroyw man, Captain Gwenlyn Jones, who is mentioned later on in our story.

The master was in overall command, and made all the key decisions. He was responsible for leaving and entering harbour, completingthe voyages safely, and conducting the company's business with the buyers or their agents.

The captain's right-hand man, the mate,made sure the vessel was loaded properly, and safely secured for sea. He was also responsible for the maintenance of the rigging, cargo gear and paintwork. The successive mates aboard the Point of Ayr were Hugh Thomas, Tom Jones (both Amlwch men), Bob Hutton of Connah's Quay, and a Bangor man whose name eludes me.

Mates aboard the *Talacre* included Gwenlyn Jones of Ffynnongroyw, Elwyn Jones of Mostyn and Ken Williams, the son of CaptainCharles Williams. Tom Vernon of Ffynnongroyw was mate of the *Tanlan* for many years. When he swallowed the anchor to become the harbour boatman, James Thomas succeeded him as mate of the *Tanlan,* followed by Mr. Downing of Birkenhead.

Elwyn Jones was in the Royal Navy during WW2 , ahero of the Normandy landings.   Courtesy Allan Jones

A good engine room crew was vital. Three men made up the 'down-below' team aboard each vessel, being the chief engineer, his second engineer and the fireman. The longstanding chief of the *Point of Ayr* was the highly competent Holywell man, Charles Dennis, mentioned above. My own father, Howell Davies, was his second for twenty-six year, taking over from a Bangor man,

John Hughes. They were followed by John Hughes' son Emlyn, and Walter Jones of Ffynnongroyw.   Another Bangor man, Richard Llewelyn,was Chief Engineer of of the *Talacre*, with Bob Lloyd of Ffynnongroyw his second. They were followed by yet another Bangor man, Chief Engineer, Maurice Pritchard.

Howell Davies,   *Author's Family Archive*

The Chief Engineer of the *Tanlan* was Theodore Wilmof. Better known as Jack, he was a native of Riga, the capital city of Latvia. He wasa jovial character who was said always to wake up laughing, and loved the British Isles dearly, frequentely praising the quality of life he had found here. He had a special soft spot for Wales, his wife, Elizabeth being from New Quay in Cardiganshire.

Like his captain, Jack Wilmof had been aboard the *Tanlan* through three names and owners, as had his second engineer, James Kelly, a Belfast man who settled in Birkenhead when Spillers the bakers bought the vessel. Sam Andrews was also a Birkenead man who came with the *Tanlan* from Spillers, and sailed aboard heras both able seaman and fireman for years.

Jobs aboard the Point boats were assidiously pursued by local seamen. Bill Dowell, grandson of Edward Blythin of the Lighthouse Cottages, Jack Whittle of Ffynnongroyw, Tom Parry of Gronant and the Mostyn brothers John and David Matthews (John later became a shipowner) all sailed in the Point boats, whilstDick Lumbourg and Tom Fish were from Connah's Quay.

The Vernon family of Ffynnongroyw produced several generations of seafarers. Tom's brothers, Joe and Frank sailed aboard the *Point of Ayr* and *Tanlan* respectively. Joe had been mentioned in despatches whilst in the Royal Navy during the first World War, and was decorated for his role in saving the crew of the motor vessel *Red Hand* when she capsized in the Hilbre Swatchway. Joe was a competent violinist and led and trained a trio aboard the *Point of Ayr*, including my father on the mandolin. Also a good pianist, his services were welcomed in watering holes both sides of the Irish Sea.

Harold Roberts of Ffynnongroyw was also decorated for his part in saving the crew of the *Red Hand*, and often sailedaboard both Coppacks' and the colliery's vessels. They are seen below when shipmates aboard Coppacks' steamer *Rosabelle,*another frequent visitor to the Point Harbour.

Joe Vernon and Harold Roberts   *Author's Family Archive*

Many crew members were from the counties of Caernarfon and Ynys Mon. John Owens, Johnny Ashton, and Captain James Thomas' brother, William were Amlwch men, whilst Glyn Tinsley, Dyfed Williams, Tom Morgan and Ken Lloyd all hailed from Yr Felinheli (Port Dinorwic).

William Thomas Courtesy Dorothy Jones

Like Sam Andrews, Eric Tinman, Dave Scanlon, Bert Lunt, and Steve Perry were Merseysiders, whilst Archie Bates hailed from Northwich. Vic Southgate a London man, also came to Ffynnongroyw via the Point boats, having been a gunner aboard the *Talacre* during the Second World war. There was also the occasional Irishman, like Kevin Duggan of Moville in County Donegal. There is no simple answer to our question of why men chose such a cruel life. Life was hard between the two world wars, and many men had few choices. The local seafarers appreciated the opportunity of being at home one or two nights a fortnight. Tom Jones and Bill Thomas found it better than whaling, and some deep-sea sailors preferred to control their

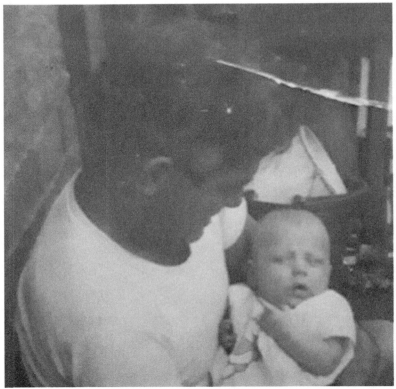

Eric Tinman with his grandchild   *Courtesy Beryl Hayes*

own diet, rather than trust crooked stewards who lined their own pockets rather than crews' stomachs. The little colliers were roughbut offered a warm camaraderie. Even when shore-side work opportunities arose, many men stayed aboard the Point vesselshaving simply become accustomed to the lifestyle.

Above: Not a flattering photograph, but both Tom Vernon (left) and Jack Whittle sailed aboard the Point boats. They were also neighbours Photograph courtesy Julie Pearson
Below: Captain Charles Williams in casual attire. Courtesy Allan Jones

PART SIX

THE END OF SEABORNE EXPORTS FROM THE POINT

Three factors came together to bring seaborne exports from the Point of Ayr to an end. Firstly, nationalisation had created a new vision for the coal industry as a U.K. national enterprise. The Point of Ayr Colliery had developed its own little niche in trading with smallish brokers and merchants across the Irish Sea. It was now part of a bigger picture. Capital was available to increase production massively, and the Irish trade began to look like small beer. Secondly, the harbour was problematic and thirdly, from a commercial viewpoint the ships were simply ageing plant, obsolete and wasteful of resources. Part Six discusses the end.

Following nationalisation, a protracted period of litigationover the ownership of the harbour and vessels impacted both badly. The Coal Board won the case, but the shipping side of the business had become uneconomical. The approaches from seaward had been badly maintained and the gutter, once a straight channel, had developed awkward bends, reducing accessibility on small tides.

The Unit Engineer, Jack Hughes, a man of vision and initiative did much to salvage the harbour situation, building a modern quay and using bulldozers to improve the channel. However, the vessels were now antiquated, and the Irish trade was becoming less profitable than alternative outlets.

On the 27th July 1958, the *Tanlan*went to Haulboline near Cork to be broken up. Her master, Captain Lamb, was too upset to take her, so Captain James Thomas of the *Point of Ayr* undertook the voyage. On the 6th October, Captain Thomas took his own ship to breakers in Rotterdam and on 24th April the followingyear, Captain Charles Williams delivered the *Talacre*'slast cargo to Drogheda before taking his ship to breakers in Dublin. The Irish trade, the mainstay of the point for seventy years ceased to exist.

An experimental re-opening was attempted in 1963. Captain Gwenlyn Jones of Ffynnongroyw, berthed the motor vessel *Indorita,* at the Point, and took 250 tons out successfully, despite the lack of either buoys or perches to mark the gutter. Captain Jones knew the estuary well. As well as being mate of the Talacre for many years, he had been relief master for the colliery ships before leaving to take command of Gardener's *Mountcharles.* Whilst anchored in the Wild Road, he launched his ship's boat at low water, and surveyed the channel, taking bearings on local landmarks. A perch was erected at his recommendation.

Captain Gwenlyn Jones   *Courtesy Pat Gonsalves Jones*

The Indorita loading at the jetty.   Courtesy of The Chester Chronicle

With the benefit of Captain Jones' survey and the perch, early in October, Captain Fernleigh (Frank) Sweet successfully berthed Coppack'smotor vessel, *Normanby Hall*, seen on p. 45. I was an able seaman aboard, and well remember the experience.

We were assisted by the colliery's boat, the *Valerie*, manned by Ken Williams, Jack Hughes, the Unit Mechanical Engineer, and his son John. Nearly forty feet longer than the *Indorita,* the *Normanby Hall* found the hidden bends in the channel a problem. Crossing the tide, she was set down onto the bank, and needed a couple of hearty nudges from the *Valerie* to keep her in the channel. The last dislodged the *Valerie's* battery, which flew forward and damaged the sea-cock. The boat began to fill up, but the crew managed to beach her before she sank.

Captain Fernleigh(Frank) Sweet   *Courtesy Haydn Sweet*

The *Normanby Hall* berthedsuccessfullyand took 375 tons of Point coal to Peel in the Isle of Man.Sadly, the revival of seaborne exports from the Point was not to be. The project was abandoned, leaving me able to say that I took the last cargo out of my home port of Point of Ayr. An era had truly come to an end,

AFTERWORD

The quay is now but an interesting historical artefact on the north-western corner of the Wales coastal path, but the mooring bollards are incorporated into the monument which commemorates the Point of Ayr Colliery. A committee was formed in March 2011to preserveand restore Number One headgear.   Local   fundraising   and   donations,   along withgrants from Cadwyn and the Lottery brought the vision into fruition in 2015.The Committee was:John Wiltshire (Chair); Michael Jones (Secretary and Project Manager, who drew up the initial design and salvaged the bollards); Alan Jones (Treasurer);IslwynLuke, Claire Harrington, David BridgeandCharlie MacDonald.
Councillor Glyn Banks was the site supervisor.

PhotographCourtesy Mike Lewis

This old esturial marker buoy was donated by the Port of Mostyn to Flintshire County Council as a landmark on the Wales Coastal Path at the site of the colliery harbour.
Photograph Courtesy John Alan Jones

BIBLIOGRAPHY

Coppack, Tom (1973), A Lifetime with Ships. T. Stephenson and Sons.

Davies, K. (1972),*The growth and development of population in Flintshire1851-1891 (Part II)*. In Flintshire Historical Society Journal 24.

Davies, W. Ken (2011), *Shipping in the Dee and Clwyd Estuaries on Census Night, 5th April,1891*. In Maritime Wales/Cymru a'rMor, THIRTYTWO.

D'Oliveira, B., and Goulder, B (Eds.) (2000). The Macmillan Reed's Nautical Amanac.

Kilgour, Owen F.G. (2008), Caernarfonshire Sail. GwasgGarregGwalch.

R.S. Fenton (1989), Cambrian Coasters: Steam and Motor Coaster Owners of North and West Wales. World Ship Society, Gravesend.

R.S. Fenton (1997), Mersey Rovers: The coastal tramp ship owners of Liverpool and the Mersey. World Ship Society, Gravesend.

Roy Fenton (2011), Coasters: An Illustrated History. Seaforth Publishing.

Gruffydd, K.Lloyd (1981),*Cyfraniad Sir Fflint: FasnachForwrol Caer, 1565 – 1800.*In Cymru a'rMor/Maritime Wales SIX.

Gruffydd,K.Lloyd (1984),*Ships and Sailors of the Dee 1277-1737*. In Cymru a'rMor/Maritime Wales EIGHT.

Gruffydd,K.Lloyd (1990),*Y Llongyn y CanolOesoedd*. In Cymru a'rMor/Maritime Wales THIRTEEN.

Gruffydd, K. Lloyd (1996), *The export of Flintshire coal before the industrial revolution*. Flintshire Historical Society Journal, 34.

Gruffydd, K.Lloyd (2000),*Export Trade in the Late Middle Ages*. In Cymru a'rMor/Maritime Wales,TWENTY ONE.

Gruffydd,K.Lloyd (2010),*Coalmining in Flintshire during the Early Modern period.* In The Flintshire Historical Society Journal, 38.

Hawson, (1954) Composite map: Talacre Harbour Company, Flint.1839-1952. D/LA/97

Jowett, Nick, (2015), Great Orme Bronze Age Mines.

Lloyd, George (1967/8), *The Canalisation of the River Dee.* In The Flintshire Historical Society Journal 23.

McGrail, Sean (2014), Early Ships and Seafaring. Pen & Sword Books.

More, Captain James (2000), Article in *Newtownwards Chronicle* on the sinking of the steamship Upas.

O'Toole, Jim. Account of the sinking of s.s. Clwyd:historypoints.org

Roberts, R. Fred *(1991). Ships built on the River Clwyd.* InCymrua'rMor/Maritime Wales,FOURTEEN

Stammers, M.K.(2000), *The Welsh Sloop.* In Cymru a'rMor/Maritime Wales,TWENTY ONE

Stammers, M.K. (1993), Mersey Flats and Flatmen. Terence Dalton Limited and National Museum and Galleries, Merseyside.

Stewart, W.K & Stephen, J.W.: Modern Chartwork; Brown, Son & Ferguson Ltd. Glasgow.

Williams, Howard M.R. (2020)Whitford Vikings? Archodaeth

Williams, C.R. (Ed. 1961) The History of Flintshire Vol. 1. Gee and Son Ltd. Denbigh.

Other publications by W. Ken Davies

W. Ken Davies: Ffynnongroyw and District: A brief journey through Time, 2020 (Illustrated Book 100 pp text and 100 illustrations) ISBN 9781527259256

Ken Davies: Science and Spirituality: In *Denumine* (Newsletter of the Alistair Harvey Trust) Autumn 2018.

Ken Davies: Chasing the Tide. A novel about intrigue, love and learning. 2016 ISBN 9781537605908.

W. Ken Davies: The lost three months of the schooner *James* of Llanelli – a maritime mystery. in Maritime Wales/Cymru a'rMorTHIRTY SIX, 2015.

Ken Davies: Maritime Activity and the Flintshire Economy in 1891Flintshire Historical Society Journal Vol. 39 2012.

Ken Davies: Shipping in the Dee and Clwyd Estuaries on Census Night, 5th April, 1891Maritime Wales/Cymru a'rMor Number THIRTY TWO2011

Ken Davies: Trade between the Mersey, Dee and Clwyd estuaries in 1891in The Liverpool Maritime Research Society Bulletin Vol. 54 No.3 December 2010.

Ken Davies: Life Aboard Two Latter Day Chester River Coasters. In Maritime Wales/Cymru a'rMor Number Thirty 2009. Also in The Maritime Research Society Bulletin Vol. 51 March & Vol.52 June 2008.

W. K. Davies: Ffynnongroyw in 1901: a proletarian village at a linguistic crossroads.Flintshire Historical Society Journal Vol. 2008

Ken Davies: Numerous articles relating to Social Care in 'Llais', the journal of the Standing Conference of Voluntary Organisations (Learning Disabilities in Wales. 1988-1996.

W.K. Davies: Client Participation in Mental Handicap Services' (with Dr. J. Øvretveit, Brunel).Develops models of client participation. in Health Service Management (October 1988).

'The Ones That Got Away' Report on a Community Initiative in Basic Adult Education.InYouth in Society (December 1983)

W.K. Davies: Review article on G. Lloyd 'Deprivation and the Bilingual Child'In 'Polyglot' Microfische Journal on Multilingualism 1978 .

W.K. Davies: 'What Did We Achieve?' Review of the 1960 Seamen's Strike. In 'The Fo'c'sle' (Magazine of the National Seamen'sReform Movement) 1962

Cover Illustrations:

<u>Front Cover:</u>

Howell Davies with his niece, Eirlys Davies, on the bridge of the steam- ship Point of Ayr ca 1954.
Author's Family Archive

Point of Ayr Harbour in early twentieth Century.
Author's Family Archive

<u>Back Cover:</u>

A view of The Point of Ayr from Picton.
Courtesy Yvonne Robert

Steam-ship Point of Ayr berthing at Carreg y Llam.
Author's Family Archive

William Thomas, seafarer. Courtesy Dorothy Jones

Captain James Thomas. Courtesy Lisa Jones

Cover design by iesfutures.com

Printed in Great Britain
by Amazon

82367853R00051